# PICTORIAL REVIEW

# PICTORIAL REVIEW

## The Demolition of Building 1515

### West Palm Beach, Florida

Dennis Johnson

**To order additional copies of this book, contact:**
Xlibris Corporation
1-888-795-4274
www.Xlibris.com
Orders@Xlibris.com
82273

# FOREWARD for Dennis Johnson

I remember the day of the demolition very well. It was a crisp February morning and the streets were crowded with people coming from across South Florida to watch the big event. News helicopters hovered above while local and network reporters swarmed the area looking for the best angles. Everyone was cautiously optimistic but we really did not know exactly what to expect. I had my staff, including construction services, City Manager, Police and Fire, and Public Information Officers on site at a command center. When the horns blew and the ground shook we watched closely as within seconds, a longstanding eyesore was reduced to a perfect pile of rubble. No injuries . . . no damage, a textbook demolition!

The 1515 Flagler building and its demise are now part of West Palm Beach history. I commend Mr.Johnson for his efforts to document and preserve the moment from this noteworthy event which forever leaves its mark on our skyline.

Mayor Lois J. Frankel-
City of West Palm Beach,
Florida 33401

## DEDICATION PAGE

TO ALL THE UNIT OWNERS WHO HAD TO ABANDON THEIR HOMES AFTER HURRICANES FRANCES AND JEANNE STRUCK IN SEPTEMBER 2004. THEY HAD TO ENDURE FINANCIAL LOSS AND A SPECTACULAR WATER VIEW. BUT CHANGE AND CHALLENGE IN LIFE IS CERTAIN, OFTEN CREATING STRENGTH AND BEAUTY.

Dennis L. Johnson, Resident
Norton Park Place
1501 South Flagler Drive
West Palm Beach, Fl 33401

# CONTENTS

# A PROLOGUE TO BUILDING 1515

After the strong winds of Hurricane Frances and Jeanne blew through and devastated the façade of Tower 1515 Condominium in September of 2004, all residents had to evacuate their building. Frances was the first hurricane to officially strike Palm Beach County in twenty-five years. Three weeks later, Jeanne struck in nearly the same place causing more damage to the building on 1515 South Flagler Drive, West Palm Beach, Florida. An assessment of the building's condition was not good. It was declared unlivable and condemned. On short notice, owners had to find temporary living quarters in nearby condominiums, apartment rentals, motels, with friends, or back to other locations throughout the United States.

The thirty-story building was built and occupied in 1974. It was called "Arkona" and was one of the most-talked about condominiums in the Palm Beaches. In 1975, it changed its name to The Tower 1515.

Many attempts were made to refurbish the building after the 2004 hurricane season to make it a livable/viable piece of real estate, but a lack of financial backing from banks and poor insurance reimbursement made it impossible to do so. The building became derelict and an eyesore to the neighborhood during the next six years.

It all came to an end at 9:03 Sunday morning (Valentine's Day), February 14, 2010. It took less than nine seconds to bring down the thirty-story building in a cloud of white smoke, depositing a forty-three-foot pile of rubble in the middle of the 2.46 acre site. It was a perfect implosion.

The $300,000 implosion project was an outstanding success due to the expertise of Advanced Explosives Demolition, Inc., of Coeur D' Alene, Idaho. Owners Eric and Lisa Kelly deserve praise and recognition for their knowledge, experience and integrity. They demonstrated concern and compassion for the surrounding neighborhood, buildings, residents, and the environment.

The project was initiated and sponsored by Trinity Development Group, LLC, in New York with Paul Grillo, President, and planners Eric Schneider and Jerry Kilday. The project gained approval after many months of work and hours of time. Many thanks go to West Palm Beach Mayor Lois J. Frankel, the City Commissioners, and the residents and managers of the surrounding neighborhoods for asking appropriate questions and listening patiently when the developer made multiple changes and requests.

The BG Group of Boca Raton worked long hours to prepare the site for demolition by removing the exterior of the building. After the implosion, they cleared all the rubble in a timely and safe manner.

Many people assisted in disseminating information to the residents and community neighbors and I would like to thank and name the following: Terri Shapleigh, Manager, of Norton Park Place, prepared reports for her building and shared communications with other buildings. Jeanine Heidtman, Rapallo North, who did a masterful job in writing weekly columns for THE CONDO NEWS regarding laws and agendas, PALM BEACH POST staff writers Collins and Abramson and THE PALM BEACH DAILY NEWS Christopher Paine for providing excellent coverage on the demise of Building 1515, Claudia and Bill Peterson for providing me an excellent view from their eighteenth floor apartment in the Trianon to photograph the early morning implosion, and my special "editor friend" Ann Logsdon who tolerates my interest in documenting and photographing endless projects.

Dennis Johnson

A PARTIAL VIEW OF PALM BEACH ATLANTIC UNIVERSITY CAMPUS AND WEST PALM BEACH COLORFUL SKYLINE TO THE NORTHWEST.

The Tower 1515
1974-2003—29 years—Active Condo Living
2004-2010—6 years—Vacant Building

(Building 1515)

(Rapallo South)

(Rapallo North)

(Norton Park Place)

(VIking arms Condo)

South Flagler Drive

14

South Rapallo               North Rapallo  Viking Arms  Building 1515  Norton Park Place

South      North      Viking     Building 1515     Norton Park Place       Trianon
Rapallo    Rapallo     Arms

**Viking Arms**        **Building 1515**        **Norton Park Place**

**Viking arms**          **Building 1515**

**Building 1515 Preparing for Demolition January 2010**

**Building 1515—Ready for Demolition**

**1501 Norton Park Place—Yellow Building—140 Feet Away**

The Perfect Implosion—February 14, 2010—First Implosion—9:03 a.m.

The Perfect Implosion—February 14, 2010—Second Implosion—9:05 a.m.

**The White Cloud Of Dust Drifted East Over The Intracoastal Waterway**

**Building 1515—February 12, 2010—Before Implosion**

**Building 1515—February 15, 2010—Day After Implosion**

**Forty-Three-Foot Pile Of Rubble On 2.46 Acre Lot—February 17, 2010**

**Technology Comes In Different Shapes And Sizes**

April 16, 2010—The 2.46 Acre Site is Clean And Ready For Green Space

27

**BG Group Of BOCA RATON—Site Clean-up On Schedule**

**BG Group BOCA RATON—April 16, 2010—Site Clean-up Completed "Flat As A Table Top"**

(MACCRANELS ORTHODONTICS)

April 16, 2010—The 2.46 Acre Site Is clean And Ready For Green Space

(Viking Arms Condominium

(MCCRANELS ORTHODONTICS
220 Arkona Court
West Palm Beach, FL 33401)

(Building 1515—West Parking Lot)

(Arkona Court—Facing West)

(Norton Park Place)

## BRAVERY IN A CONSTRUCTION ZONE

IN THE SHADOW OF BUILDING 1515 AND VERY CLOSE TO GROUND "ZERO" MCCRANELS ORTHODONTICS HAS ENDURED MANY INCONVENIENCES FROM THE DERELICT BUILDING. I COMMEND THEM FOR AN ACT OF BRAVERY UNDER THE CONDITIONS OF A THIRTY-STORY BUILDING BEING IMPLODED WITHIN 85 FEET, THE SMOKE AND DEBRIS FLYING IN EVERY DIRECTION, CONSTANT NOISE OF DUMP TRUCKS, GIANT FRONT-END LOADERS AND CAT EXCAVATORS REMOVING CHUNKS OF CONCRETE AND REBAR FROM THE FORTY-THREE-FOOT PILE OF RUBBLE. SPECTATORS WALKING ACROSS THE FRONT AND BACK END OF THEIR PROPERTY. AND THE CLEAN-UP PROCESS WILL BE ON-GOING FOR MONTHS. DUE TO THE PERFECT IMPLOSION, THEY WERE SPARED FROM ANY SERIOUS DAMAGE TO THEIR STRUCTURE. NORTON PARK PLACE AND VIKING ARMS ENDURED THE SAME STRESS OF PRE-DEMOLITION PREPARATIONS, DEMOLITION VIA IMPLOSION, AND POST CLEAN-UP TO BE COMPLETED BY MAY 2010.

# BUILDING 1515

One of the Third- Tallest Implosions Staged
in the United States.

**Building 1515 - The facade of a derelict structure after the 2004 hurricanes.**

**Building 1515 has been stripped of all plumbing and
electrical fixtures in preparation for demolition.**

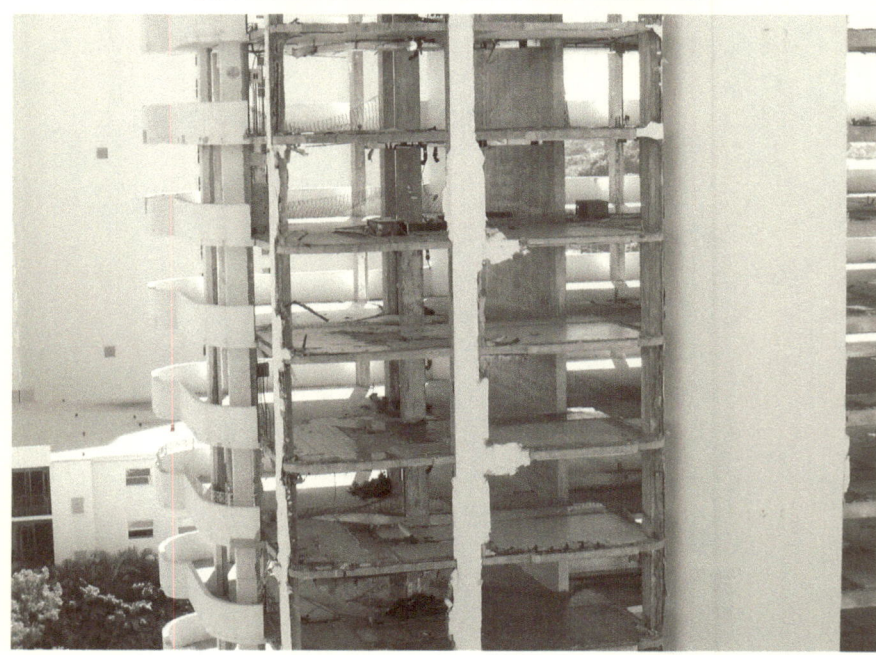

**Bird's eye view of the massive project for the BG Group-Boca Raton to prepare for demolition.**

**Building 1515 - The southwest corner was the starting point for the removal of asbestos materials at various locations within the building.**

**Building 1515–The southeast corner was the starting point for the removal of the outside brick and mortar exposing the stairwells– bottom to top – 30 stories.**

**BG Group engaged in massive clean-up on site – sorting and saving
the rebar from the concrete by the truck loads.**

**Clean-up detail of Building 1515 on 2.46 acre site**

**Trucking out the debris to an off-site landfill**

The end of the rubble is near for the massive clean-up on site

A close up of the rebar removed from the concrete
before it is hauled away to the landfill.

**West end of 2.46 acre site during the final days of the project.**

East end of 2.46 acre site during the final days of the project.

**BG Group workers climbing up the mountain of rubble**

**BG Group - King of Hill - The demise of Building 1515**

**Photographer Dennis Johnson with his Minolta Maxxum/Dynax 5 camera and zoom lens (real film - not digital) on tripod to take the implosion of building 1515.**

Thru the photographer's view finder you can find the target site after the building was imploded and pancaked down to the ground and to the roar of the spectators.